This book
belongs to:

A Prayer a Day

This edition published by Parragon Books Ltd in 2015 and distributed by

Parragon Inc.
440 Park Avenue South, 13th Floor
New York, NY 10016
www.parragon.com

Original prayers by Meryl Doney and Jan Payne
Cover illustrated by Alessandra Psacharopulo and Veronica Vasylenko
Prayers illustrated by Jayne Church and Stuart Trotter

ISBN 978-1-4748-3138-3

Printed in China

A Prayer a Day

Parragon

Bath • New York • Cologne • Melbourne • Delhi
Hong Kong • Shenzhen • Singapore • Amsterdam

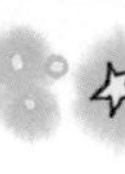

Contents

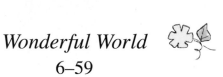

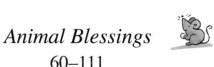

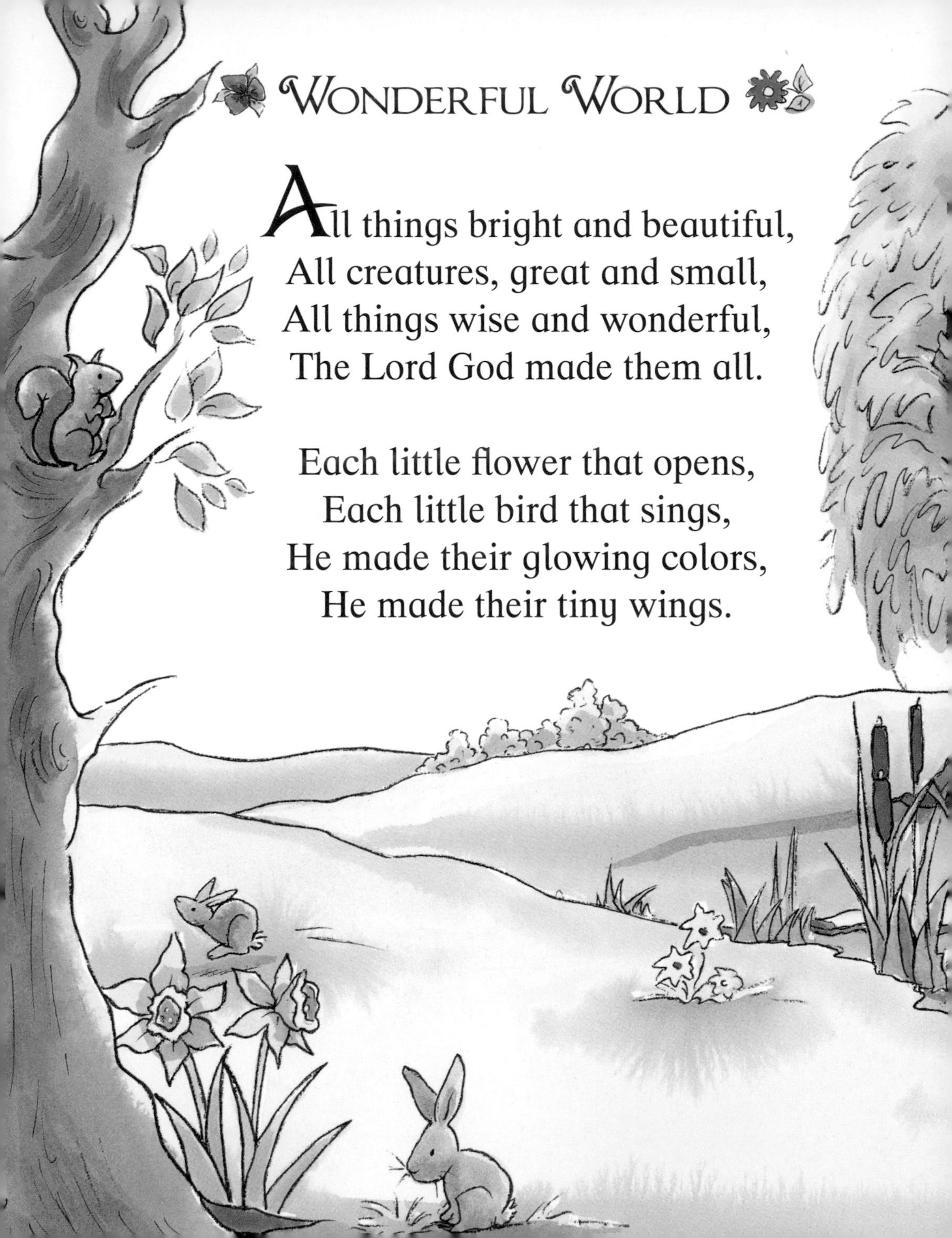

Wonderful World

All things bright and beautiful,
All creatures, great and small,
All things wise and wonderful,
The Lord God made them all.

Each little flower that opens,
Each little bird that sings,
He made their glowing colors,
He made their tiny wings.

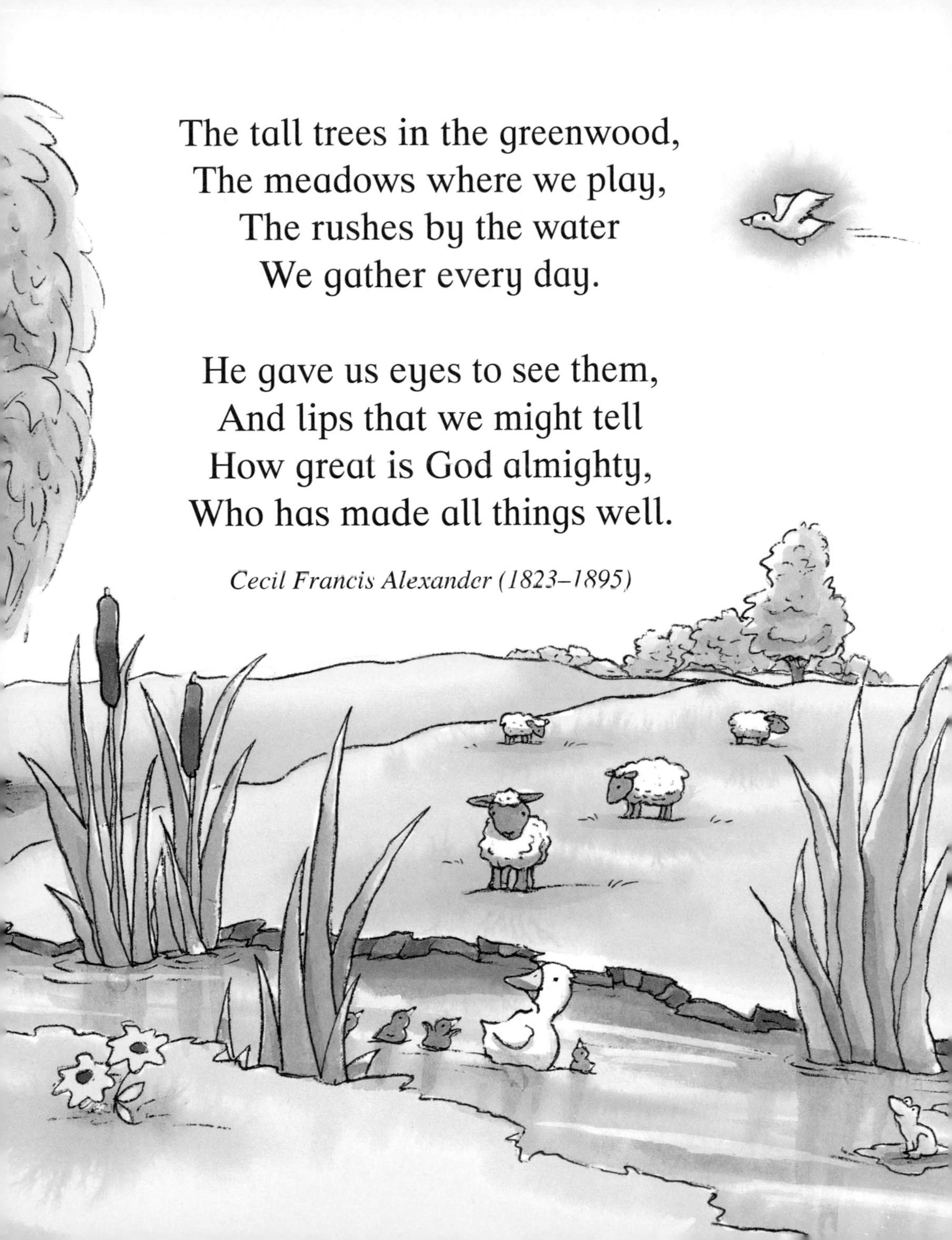

The tall trees in the greenwood,
The meadows where we play,
The rushes by the water
We gather every day.

He gave us eyes to see them,
And lips that we might tell
How great is God almighty,
Who has made all things well.

Cecil Francis Alexander (1823–1895)

Thank you, God, for showing me
The perfect beauty of a tree.
I didn't know a tree could be
Remarkable, like you and me.

God made the world so broad and grand,
Filled with blessings from his hand.
He made the sky so high and blue,
And all the little children, too.

Anonymous

For every bright green leaf unfurled,
Thank you, God—what a wonderful world!

In the beginning, God looked at everything that he had made and he saw that it was very good. When I look at the world I say, "Thank you, God, for making it very, very good."

Dear God, bless our nets as we cast and trawl;
The ocean is deep and our ship is small.

Traditional

For this new morning and its light,
For rest and shelter of the night,
For health and food, for love and friends,
For every gift your goodness sends,
We thank you, gracious Lord.

Anonymous

Bright is the morning,
New is the day;
When I wake,
To God I say—
"Good morning!"

Cool is the evening,
At close of day;
Before I sleep,
To God I say—
"Good night!"

Dear God,
I like grass.
It grows and grows.
It tickles me
Between my toes.
It's like a carpet
Spread for me.
And it's as green
As green can be.

For flowers that bloom about our feet,
Father we thank thee.
For tender grass so fresh, so sweet,
Father we thank thee.
For the bird and hum of bee,
For all things fair we hear or see,
Father in heaven, we thank thee.

Ralph Waldo Emerson (1803–1882)

When astronauts look back at our world from the moon, they see that it is beautiful—blue and green and white with clouds. Help us keep our world clean and beautiful because it's such a special place.

For a million stars that sparkle
In a sky of darkest blue—
I cannot count the stars,
But, God, I can thank you.

For air and sunshine, pure and sweet,
We thank our heavenly Father;
For grass that grows beneath our feet,
We thank our heavenly Father;
For lovely flowers the hedge along,
For graceful trees with branches strong,
For birds that sing their joyful song,
We thank our heavenly Father.

Anonymous

The green land stretches to the sea
and we who live on it can travel
and enjoy the lanes and hills,
the sheep and goats and cows,
the streams and rocks, the beaches
and the sand. We thank you, God,
for this good land.

Tomorrow is a special day
I'm off on vacation—hooray!
I'm going where there's sand and sea,
And lots of treats for you and me.
Where ponies give rides on the beach,
And seagulls fly just out of reach.

Dear God,
Thank you for the sun so bright
That fills the world with dazzling light.
And thank you for the muffled sound
When snow lies thickly on the ground.

A special thanks for gentle rain,
Which helps the grass grow green again.
But please, God, send the wind, I pray
So I can fly my kite today.

The year's at the spring;
the day's at the morn;
morning's at seven;
the hill-side's dew-pearled;
the lark's on the wing;
the snail's on the thorn;
God's in his heaven—
all's right with the world!

Robert Browning (1812–1889)

Dear God,
I know it's spring
When I hear the birds sing.
They're thanking you
For making things new.

Summer suns are glowing
Over land and sea,
Happy light is flowing
Bountiful and free.
Everything rejoices
In the mellow rays,
All earth's thousand voices
Swell the psalm of praise.

Bishop How (1823–1897)

I love to see the raindrops
Splashing on the sidewalks;
I love to see the sunlight
Twinkling in the rain;
I love to see the wind-gusts
Drying up the raindrops;
I love to feel the sunshine
Coming out again.

Thank you for the thunderstorm,
Thank you for the wind and rain,
And thank you for the sunshine
Coming out again.

When it rains in summer,
When the sky turns gray,
When the rain clouds gather
And I can't go out to play,
Then I see the wet grass
And it makes me think,
How glad I am that all the plants
Have lovely rain to drink!

Roses are red,
Violets are blue.
When it rains, dear God,
I thank you!

Plants need the water
Just as we do.
For sending the rain, dear God,
We thank you!

Thank you for the special time
When winds begin to blow
And golden leaves come tumbling down
Setting the earth aglow.

I know the summer's over now,
And winter's on its way,
But I am full of happiness
On this colorful, bright day.

Oh, thought I!
What a beautiful thing
God has made winter to be,
By stripping trees
And letting us see
Their shape and forms.
What a freedom does it seem
To give them to the storms.

Dorothy Wordsworth (1771–1855)

God bless the field and bless the furrow,
Stream and branch and rabbit burrow.
Bless the minnow, bless the whale,
Bless the rainbow and the hail.
Bless the nest and bless the leaf,
Bless the righteous and the thief.
Bless the wing and bless the fin,
Bless the air I travel in.
Bless the mill and bless the mouse,
Bless the miller's bricken house.
Bless the earth and bless the sea,
God bless you and God bless me.

Anonymous

Dear God,
The end of summer is sad—
But you give us apples
To make us glad!

I peeked through the curtain
When I woke in the night.
Great, gray flakes
Were an amazing sight.

I woke in the morning,
And to my delight,
All the world was
Sparkling white!

Snowdrops,
Ice drops,
Raindrops
Fall.
Sun shines down
To kiss them all.
See them sparkle in the light,
Winter's wonders
Jewel-bright.
Snowdrops,
Ice drops,
Raindrops
All,
Show God's love
For great and small.

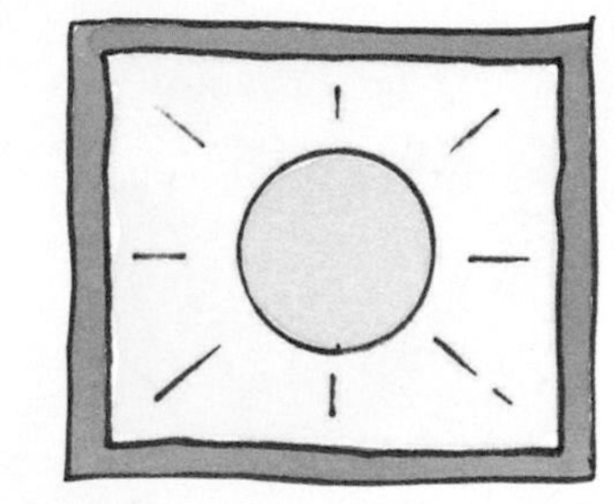

In winter, all the creatures
Shelter from the storm.
Thank you, God, for homes that keep us
Safe and warm.

Oh God! who giv'st the winter's cold,
As well as summer's joyous rays,
Us warmly in thy love enfold,
And keep us through life's wintry days.

S. Longfellow (1819–1892)

In the middle of winter
At dead of night,
That's when God was born on earth,
King of light.

Joy to the world!
The Lord is come;
Let earth receive her King;
Let every heart
Prepare him room,
And heav'n and nature sing,
And heav'n and nature sing,
And heav'n, and heav'n
And nature sing.

Joy to the world!
The Savior reigns;
Let men their songs employ,
While fields and floods,
Rocks, hills and plains
Repeat the sounding joy,
Repeat the sounding joy,
Repeat, repeat
The sounding joy.

Isaac Watts (1674–1748)

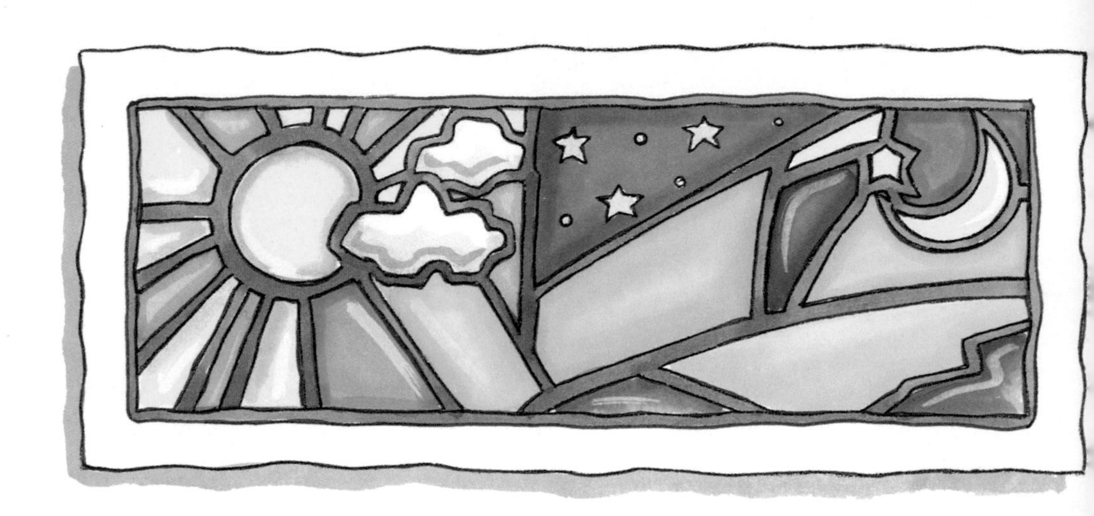

Praise the Lord! Ye heavens adore him,
Praise him, angels in the height!
Sun and moon, rejoice before him,
Praise him, all ye stars and light.

John Kempthorne (1775–1838)

We can praise God on the trumpet,
We can praise him on the drum,
We can praise him with our dancing,
We can whistle, shout or hum.
We can praise God on the violin
Or use our voice to sing,
We can make a very joyful noise
On almost anything!

Lord thy glory fills the heaven,
Earth is with its fullness stored;
Unto thee be glory given,
Holy, holy, holy Lord.

Bishop Mant (1776–1848)

Praise the Lord! Praise him on earth, praise him in heaven. Praise him for the wonderful things he has done, and just for being God.

From Psalm 150

All things praise thee, Lord most high!
Heaven and earth and sea and sky!
Time and space are praising thee!
All things praise thee; Lord, may we!

George William Conder (1821–1874)

I may be small,
But I can sing
A song of praise
To God the king.

Praise the Lord from the heavens,
praise him in the heights!
Praise him, all his angels,
praise him, all his host!

Praise him, sun and moon,
praise him, all you shining stars!
Praise him, you highest heavens,
and you waters above the heavens!

Praise the Lord from the earth,
you sea monsters and all deeps,
fire and hail, snow and frost,
stormy wind fulfilling his command!

Mountains and all hills,
fruit trees and all cedars!
Wild animals and all cattle,
creeping things and flying birds!

Kings of the earth and all peoples,
princes and all rulers of the earth!
Young men and women alike,
old and young together!

Let them praise the name of the Lord,
for his name alone is great.

From Psalm 148

Dear God, I love to be on the beach
where the sand meets the ocean.
It reminds me what a wonderful world you've made.

On the beach I can look far out
where the ocean meets the sky,
and know that there's a wonderful world out there.

Perhaps one day
I'll go traveling and see the world.

Thank you for flowers,
Thank you for trees,
Thank you for grasses
That toss in the breeze.
Thank you for vegetables,
Thank you for spice,
Thank you for everything
That makes food taste nice.
Thank you, dear Father,
For all things that grow
In sunshine and rain,
And the glowing rainbow.

Glory be to God for dappled things.

G. M. Hopkins (1844–1889)

Two eyes to see, two ears to hear,
one nose to smell, one mouth to tell.
How great is God who gave them to me.

God who made the earth,
The air, the sky, the sea,
Who gave the light its birth,
Careth for me.

Sarah Betts Rhodes (1824–1904)

Wide as the world,
(spread arms wide)

Deep as the sea,
(point down deep)

High as the sky,
(point up high)

Is your love for me.
(hug yourself)

Dear God, thank you for our town;
for all the beautiful and surprising things
we can see in the streets and gardens,
for sparkles in the sidewalk, rainbows
in the puddles, blossom petals fluttering
in the gutter, and sun glinting off the
windowpanes. They make walking
down the road an exciting journey.

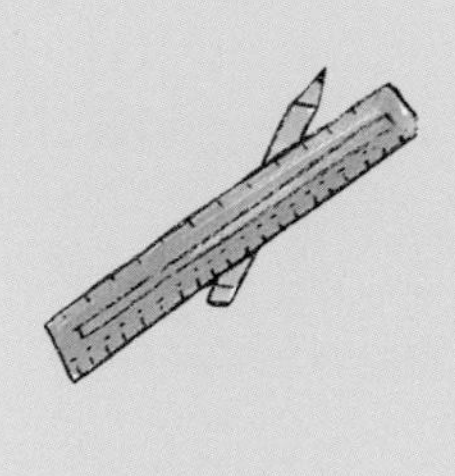

School is over.
We fold our hands, and thank
the Lord, who has been with us.

Ms Margot Damjakob (1939–1940)

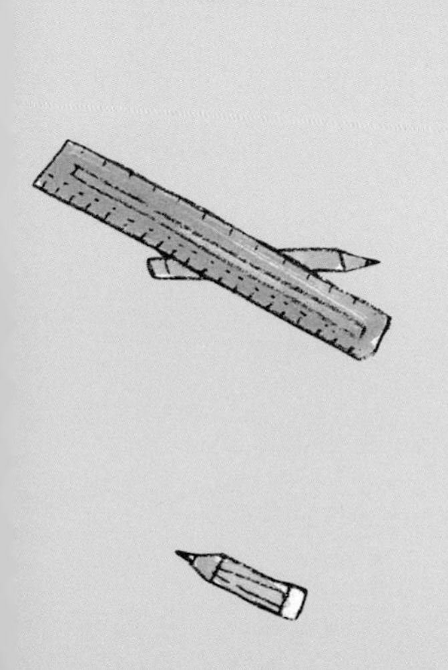

God bless everyone I know
As they go
Up and down
In our town.

God bless those I've yet to meet
And learn to greet
In road
In street.

You know them, great and small,
And love them all.

A town is made up of lots of people living together in one place. Dear God, help us make our town a good place to live.

Lord, make me see your glory
in every place.

Michelangelo (1475–1564)

When I travel in a bus I see
the streets and houses. When I go
in a train, I see the fields and hills.
When I fly in an airplane, I can see
the whole country.

If I could go up in a rocket, I would see
the whole world. Thank you, God,
for travel. It shows me what a great world
you have made.

Animal Blessings

Jesus our brother, strong and good,
Was humbly laid in a manger of wood,
And the friendly beasts around him stood,
Jesus our brother, strong and good.

"I," said the donkey, shaggy and brown,
"I carried his mother uphill and down,
I carried her safely to Bethlehem town;
I," said the donkey, shaggy and brown.

"I," said the cow, all white and red,
"I gave him my manger for his bed,
I gave him my hay to pillow his head,
I," said the cow, all white and red.

"I," said the sheep with the curly horn,
"I gave him my wool for his blanket warm,
He wore my coat on Christmas morn;
I," said the sheep with the curly horn.

"I," said the dove, from the rafters high,
"Cooed him to sleep, my mate and I;
We cooed him to sleep, my mate and I;
I," said the dove, from the rafters high.

And every beast by some good spell,
In the stable dark was glad to tell,
Of the gift he gave Immanuel,
The gift he gave Immanuel.

Traditional carol (c. 1300)

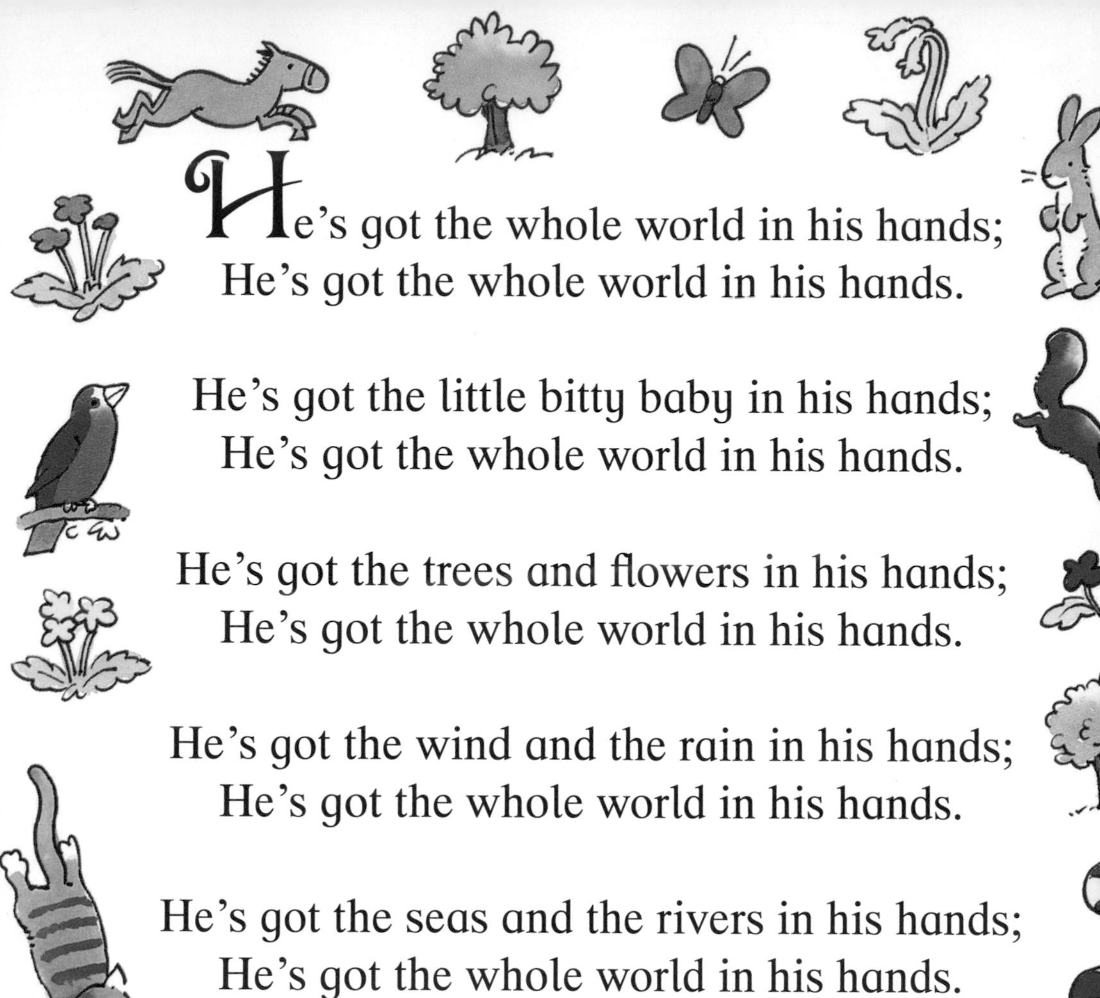

He's got the whole world in his hands;
He's got the whole world in his hands.

He's got the little bitty baby in his hands;
He's got the whole world in his hands.

He's got the trees and flowers in his hands;
He's got the whole world in his hands.

He's got the wind and the rain in his hands;
He's got the whole world in his hands.

He's got the seas and the rivers in his hands;
He's got the whole world in his hands.

He's got you and me, brother, in his hands;
He's got you and me, sister, in his hands.

He's got the whole world in his hands!

Traditional spiritual

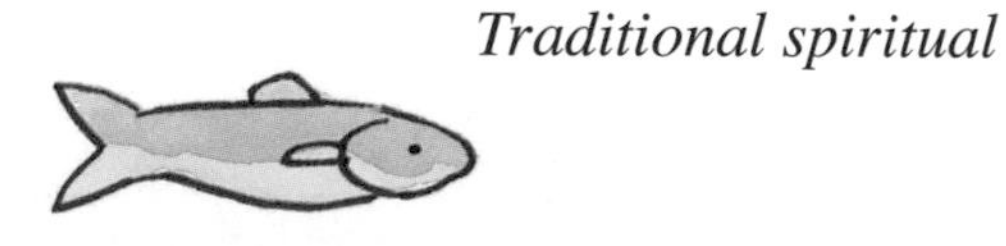

Thank you, God, that the world is wide;
that there are so many countries and
so many different people.

Thank you, God, that the seas are deep;
that the oceans are full of amazing creatures,
which swim and dive and play.

Thank you, God, that the sky is high;
that the stars we see twinkling in the night
are moving in the vast areas of space.

Thank you, God, that I'm in this wide, deep, high
world with you.

Thank you, God, for giving us
The hippo and rhinoceros.
For crazy monkeys, brash and loud,
Giraffes with heads stuck in the cloud.
Thanks for parrots bold and bright,
And zebras smart in black and white.

For elephants with giant feet,
And anteaters so trim and neat.
I wouldn't want the world to be
Empty except for you and me.

Dear God, I had some yummy honey for lunch. Then I saw a show on TV about how bees make honey, and talk to each other, and make their hive ready for winter. I was amazed at how they do it all and how busy they are. Now when I have honey I say, "Thank you bees for making honey— and thank you God for making bees."

Dear God, I heard
The song of a bird,
Singing for joy in the morning.
It made my heart sing
Like anything
That I am alive, like him.

The little cares that fretted me,
I lost them yesterday.
Among the fields, above the sea,
Among the winds at play,
Among the lowing herds,
The rustling of the trees,
Among the singing of the birds,
The humming of the bees.

The foolish fears of what might pass,
I cast them away,
Among the clover-scented grass,
Among the new-mown hay,
Among the hushing of the corn
Where the drowsy poppies nod,
Where ill thoughts die and good are born—
Out in the fields with God.

Louise Imogen Guiney (1861–1920)

Little lamb, who made thee?
Dost thou know who made thee?
Gave thee life and bade thee feed
By the stream and over the mead;
Gave thee clothing of delight,
Softest clothing, woolly, bright;
Gave thee such a tender voice
Making all the vales rejoice?
Little lamb, who made thee?
Dost thou know who made thee?

William Blake (1757–1827)

I thank God for my rabbit,
Who's soft and furry
And wiggles his nose
All the time—it's his habit.

The song of the wren,
The smallest bird,
Is the biggest and strongest
I've ever heard.
He's praising God
For his little nest,
And I think he'll burst
With happiness!

Lo, the winter is past, the rain is over and gone, the flowers appear on the earth, the time of the singing of the birds is come, and the voice of the turtle dove is heard in the land.

From The Song of Solomon

Dear God, help me to be gentle and kind to every living creature.

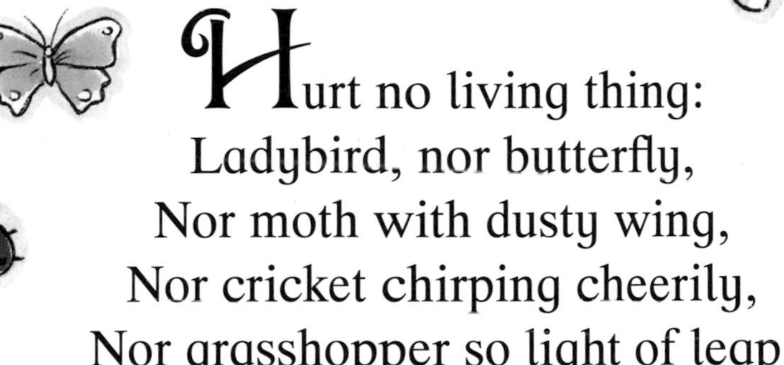

Hurt no living thing:
Ladybird, nor butterfly,
Nor moth with dusty wing,
Nor cricket chirping cheerily,
Nor grasshopper so light of leap,
Nor dancing gnat, nor beetle fat,
Nor harmless worms that creep.

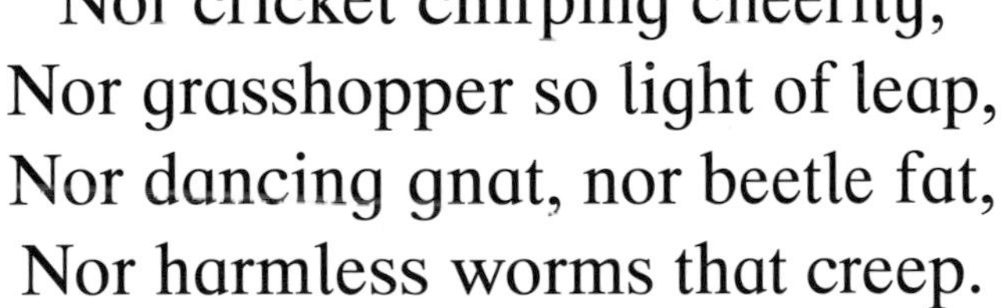

Christina Rossetti (1830–1894)

From ghoulies and ghosties,
long-leggety beasties, and things
that go bump in the night,
good Lord deliver us.

Traditional

He prayeth best, who loveth best
All things both great and small;
For the dear God who loveth us,
He made and loveth all.

Samuel Taylor Coleridge (1772–1834)

The sea is Christ's, the fishes are Christ's; in the nets of God may we all meet.

Irish prayer

We pray, Lord, for the humble beasts
who with us bear the burden and heat of the
day, giving their lives for the well-being of their
countries; and for the wild creatures, whom you
have made wise, strong, and beautiful; we ask
for them your great tenderness of heart, for you
have promised to save both man and beast,
and great is your loving-kindness,
oh Savior of the world.

Russian prayer

The worm is
very plain,
but then again
the worm is
very good
at what he does.
Without him
my garden
would not live.
So thank you, God,
for worms
And all they give.

Beetles are funny,
Ants are too,
Flies have fantastic wings.
Sometimes I like them
So my prayer is,
"Thank you, God, for the smallest things."

Spiders are scary,
Mice are too,
Moths have fluttery wings.
Sometimes I hate them
So I say, "Help me
Not to be scared of the smallest things!"

No shop does the bird use,
No counter nor baker,
But the bush is his orchard,
The grass is his acre.
The ant is his quarry,
The seed is his bread,
And a star is his candle
To light him to bed.

Elizabeth Coatsworth (1893–1986)

When dogs bark and hamsters squeak,
Are they really trying to speak?
When hens and roosters cluck and crow,
Are they really in the know?
Dear God, do animals talk to you
And tell you what they'd like to do?
For, if they can't, I'd like to say,
Please watch over them today.

Loving Shepherd of thy sheep,
Keep thy lambs, in safety keep;
Nothing can thy power withstand;
None can pluck them from thy hand.

Jane Eliza Leeson (1807–1882)

God who made lambs, look after me as one of your own flock.

The snail does
the holy will of God
slowly.

G.K. Chesterton (1874–1936)

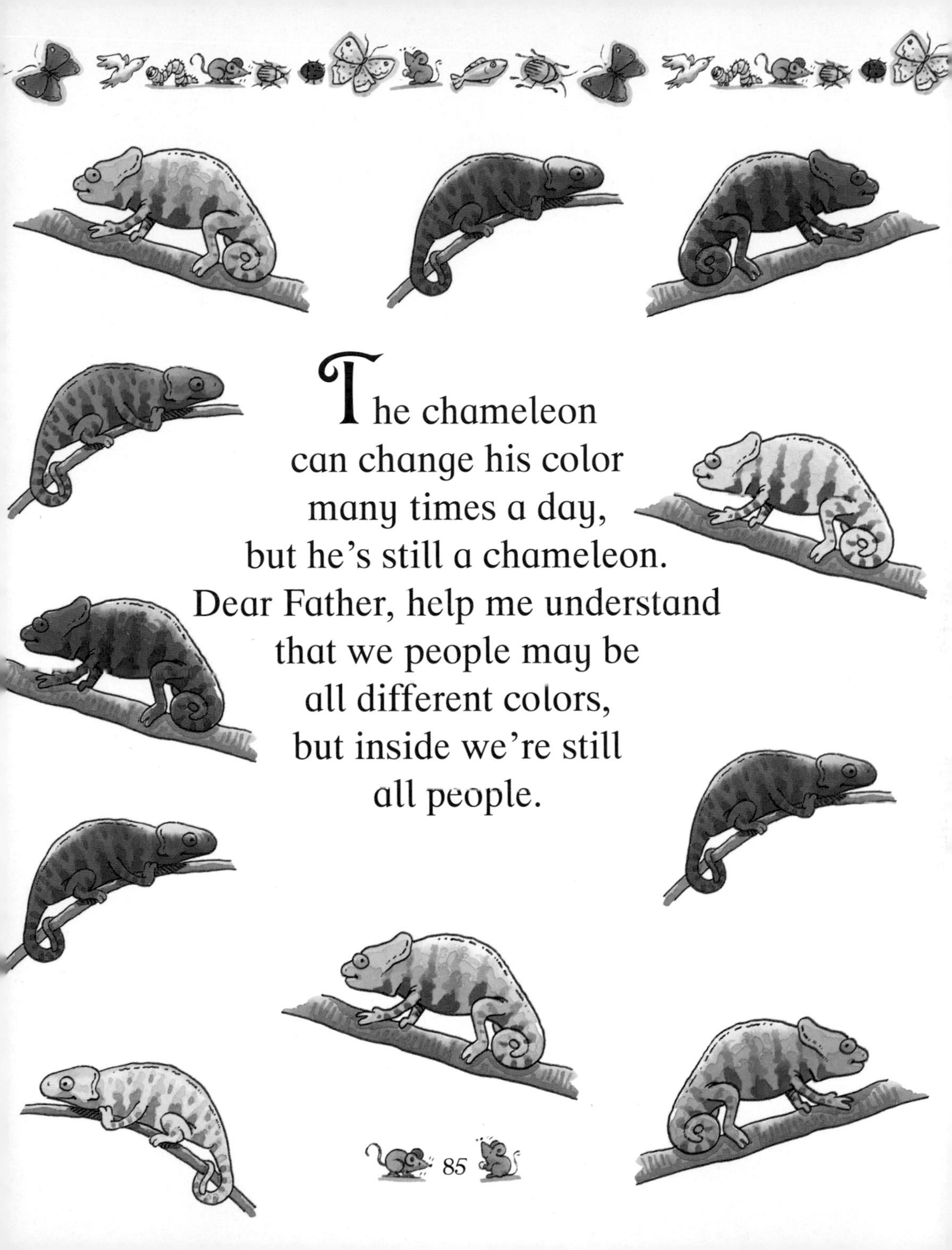

The chameleon
can change his color
many times a day,
but he's still a chameleon.
Dear Father, help me understand
that we people may be
all different colors,
but inside we're still
all people.

To all the humble beasts there be,
To all the birds on land and sea,
Great Spirit, sweet protection give
That free and happy they may live!

Thank you for the beasts so tall,
Thank you for the creatures small.
Thank you for all things that live,
Thank you, God, for all you give.

Anonymous

I heard a lark singing this morning.
He flew straight up into the blue sky,
singing for all he was worth.
Help me learn how to praise you,
Lord, as gladly as that lark.

The lark's on the wing;
the snail's on the thorn:
God's in his Heaven—
all's right with the world!

Robert Browning (1812–1889)

Dear Father, hear and bless
Thy beasts and singing birds,
And guard with tenderness
Small things that have no words.

Anonymous

I come in the little things,
saith the Lord: not borne on the
morning's wings of majesty, but I have
set my feet amidst the delicate
and bladed wheat.

I come in the little things,
saith the Lord: yea! On the glancing
wings of eager birds, the softly
pattering feet of furred and gentle beasts.

I come in the little things,
saith the Lord.

Evelyn Underhill (1875–1941)

My friend the tortoise
Doesn't say much,
He don't need a cage,
A nest, or a hutch.
He brings his own house
Wherever he goes,
Whatever he thinks about
Only God knows.

Dear God,
our pets are very special.
They give us love and
many happy hours.
They teach us how to love
and look after them.
Thank you.

I had a little puppy—
I fed him every day.
We'd play indoors
Or go for walks,
And run and jump and play.

That little puppy grew and grew
Till he was fully grown.
Now I am big
And he is too—
I thank God he's my own.

Our pets are our friends.
They let us know we're not alone.
So when they die, we are sad inside.
Help us in our sadness to remember
all the good things about our pets
and to thank you for them.

God bless the animals
Great and small,
And help us learn
To love them all.

There are so many creatures
All over the world
From the elephant to the gnu.
So many shapes
And colors and kinds,
So I say, dear God, thank you.

Here's my goldfish
Sweet and small,
She can't remember
Much at all.
So please help me
To remember
To give her food
And care for her.

Dear God,
I love to watch my gerbil running around,
eating his food, and scratching behind his ears.
Please help me look after him every day
so that he is a safe and happy gerbil.
Amen

Thank you, God, that looking after our pets reminds us how much you love us and care for us.
Amen

First we had two rabbits,
Then we had four,
After a while
We had sixteen more.
I love baby rabbits, God,
I think it's really great
That two rabbits have more rabbits,
Until there's twenty-eight!

Our little kitten
Never sleeps—
He rolls and jumps,
He runs and leaps.
But I am sure
This ball of fur
Is praising God
With every purr.

Please listen to this special prayer,
And if I start to cry,
It's because my budgie's sick
And I think he's going to die.
Nothing lives forever,
That is something I know.
But even though I know it,
I wish it wasn't so.

Please God, you know how much we love [pet's name], and now [pet's name] is not very well. Please help us look after [pet's name]. Help the vet know how to treat [pet's name] and, if possible, to make [pet's name] better again.

Me and my dog,
My dog and me,
Are just as happy as we can be.
God loves me
And God loves him—
We go together like anything.

Lord, you have made
so many things!
How wisely you made
them all! The earth
is filled with your
creatures.

From Psalm 104

Praise God, from whom all blessings flow,
Praise him, all creatures here below,
Praise him above, ye heavenly host,
Praise Father, Son, and Holy Ghost.

All creatures of our God and king,
Lift up your voice and with us sing
Alleluia, alleluia!

St. Francis of Assisi (c. 1225)

Oh heavenly Father, protect and bless all things that have breath: guard them from all evil and let them sleep in peace.

Albert Schweitzer (1875–1965)

Thank you, God, that I can break my nighttime fast with breakfast. What a great way to start a day!

Munch, munch, munch,
Thank you for our lunch.

Dear God above,
for all your love, and for
our treats, we thank you.

Thank you for my dinner,
Thank you for my friends,
Thank you for my family,
And love that never ends.

For health and strength and
daily food, we praise your name,
oh Lord.

Traditional

Bless me, oh Lord, and let my food
strengthen me to serve thee,
for Jesus' sake.

The New England Primer

For what we are about to receive
may the Lord make us truly thankful.

Anonymous

Bless us, oh Lord, and these thy gifts,
which of thy bounty we are about to receive.
Through Christ our Lord.

Traditional

Blessed art thou, Lord our God, king of the universe, who feeds the entire world in his goodness—with grace, with kindness, and with mercy. He gives food to all life, for his kindness is eternal. Blessed are you, God, who nourishes all.

Jewish blessing

Be present at our table, Lord;
Be here and everywhere adored.
Thy creatures bless, and grant that we
May feast in paradise with thee.

John Wesley (1703–1791)

Bless, dear Lord, my daily food
To make me healthy, strong and good.

School lunches can taste nasty;
School lunches can taste nice.
But I love my school lunches;
I could eat them twice!

Some days I eat up everything;
Sometimes I like to share.
Thank you for school lunches, God,
Because my friends are there.

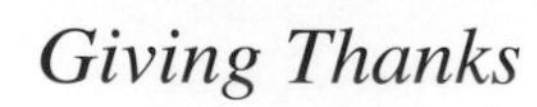

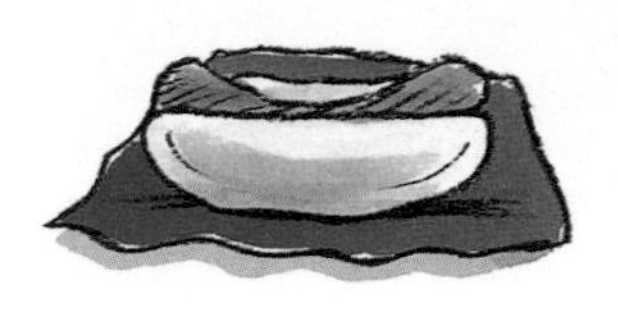

Pizzas and burgers, a plate of hot dogs,
Barbecued chicken, which everyone hogs!

Pudding and ice cream, a big birthday cake,
Gingerbread cookies, which I helped to make.

These are the things that we all love to eat.
Thank you, dear Father, for each tasty treat.

Just a glass of warm milk,
Just a slice of bread,
Thank you for these good things
On my way to bed.

Bread and water are enough
To make sure we are fed.
But it's so nice
To add to these
A little peanut butter spread!

I pray that ordinary bread,
Be just as nice as cake;
I pray that I could fall asleep,
As easy as I wake.

Anonymous

Oh, the Lord is good to me,
And so I thank the Lord
For giving me the things I need,
The sun, the rain, and the apple seed.
Oh, the Lord is good to me.

John Chapman, "Johnny Appleseed," (1774–1845)

Blessed art thou, oh Lord our God, king of the universe, who bringest forth bread from the earth.

Jewish blessing

Cows make milk
And bees make honey.
Farmers cut corn
When it's sunny.
Plums and apples
Grow on trees.
And in Dad's garden
Are beans and peas.
Thank you, God,
For the food I eat,
For fruit and milk
And bread and meat.
If it wasn't for
These gifts from you
I really don't know what we'd do!

Dear God,
Thank you for all the wonderful food
And letting me taste it.
Help me think of others, too,
And not to waste it.

Thank you, Father God, for our food,
and thank you for those who have prepared it.

Red tomato,
Orange carrot,
Yellow pepper,
Lettuce green,
Beets that have blue and purple
Indigo and violet sheen.
Thank you, God, that in my salad
Rainbow colors can be seen.

All this world is God's own field,
Fruit unto his praise to yield;
Wheat and tares together sown,
Unto joy or sorrow grown;
First the blade and then the ear,
Then the full corn shall appear:
Lord of the harvest, grant that we
Wholesome grain and pure may be.

H. Alford (1810–1871)

Dear God,
Thank you for the people
Who grew this food for me.
Thank you for the people
Who brought this food to me.
Thank you for the people
Who prepared this food for me.

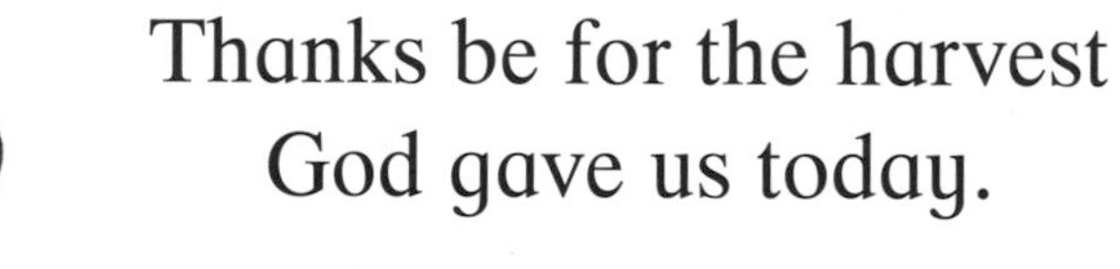

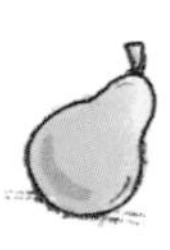

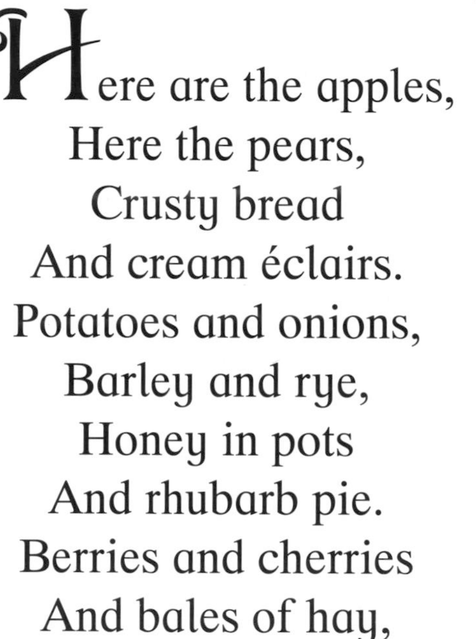

Here are the apples,
Here the pears,
Crusty bread
And cream éclairs.
Potatoes and onions,
Barley and rye,
Honey in pots
And rhubarb pie.
Berries and cherries
And bales of hay,
Thanks be for the harvest
God gave us today.

Somebody sowed it, somebody watered,
Somebody weeded and hoed,
And God gave the sun, the wind, and the rain
To bring us this harvest of food.

Father, we thank thee for this food,
For health and strength and all things good.
May others all these blessings share,
And hearts be grateful everywhere.

Traditional

Dear Jesus, who loved to
eat and drink and to share food
with your friends, be here with us
as we enjoy this meal.

Us and this; God bless.

Quaker prayer

The bread is warm and fresh,
The water cool and clear.
Lord of all life, be with us,
Lord of all life, be near.

African grace

God is great,
God is good,
Let us thank him
For this food.

Anonymous

Thank you, God,
for this day, this family,
and this food.

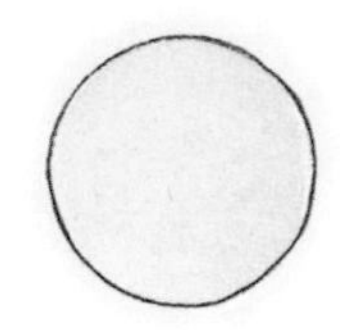

It is very nice to think
The world is full of meat and drink,
With little children saying grace
In every far-flung kind of place.

Robert Louis Stevenson (1850–1894)

Some hae meat and canna eat,
And some wad eat that want it;
But we hae meat and we can eat,
And sae the Lord be thankit.

Robert Burns (1759–1796)

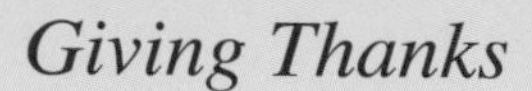

Jesus fed the multitude
On five loaves and two fishes.
We don't know how he did it
But, Jesus, bless these dishes!

Father, as we enjoy the food that gives us strength, help us remember those who have less than we do. May we pay attention to what's going on in the world and use our strength and money to help in any way we can.

Dear God,
Help me share
All that you have given me
With your children
Everywhere.

Jesus, you fed many people with only
five loaves of bread and two fishes.
Help us to share what we have with others.

May we who have much
remember those who have little.
May we who are full remember those
who are hungry. May we who are
loved remember those who are lonely.
May we who are safe remember those
who are in danger. May we who have
so much learn to share.

Dear God, thank you for
this drink of water. Thank you for its
clear sparkle, and that it is fresh and clean.
Help me remember those who have no
clean water to drink. Help us do all
we can to help them.

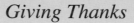

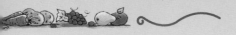

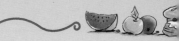

Each time we eat,
may we remember God's love.

Prayer from China

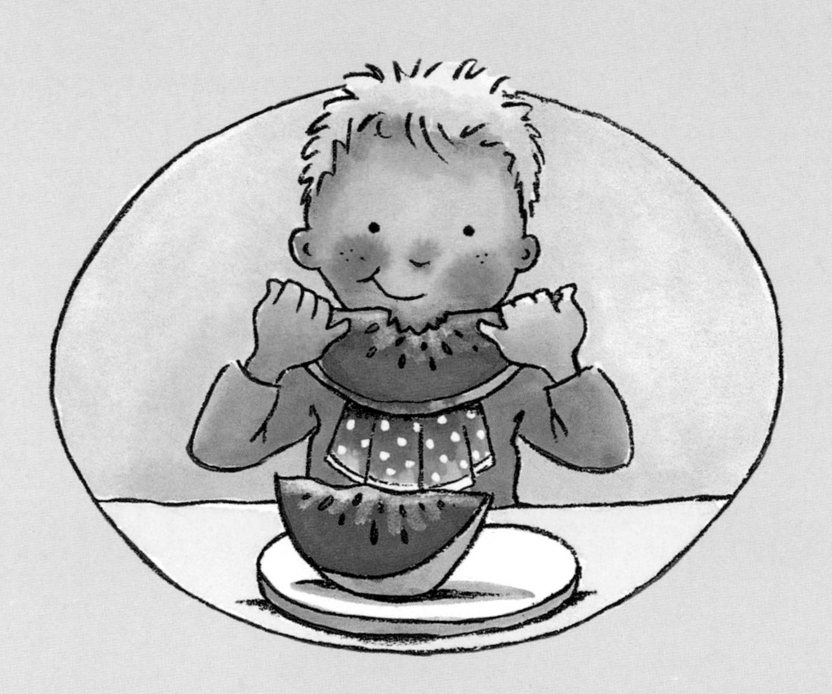

All good gifts around us,
Are sent from heaven above,
Then thank the Lord, oh thank the Lord,
For all his love.

Matthias Claudius (1740–1815)

Peace be to this house
and to all who dwell here.
Peace be to those that enter
and to those that depart.

Anonymous

Oh God, make the door of this house wide enough to receive all who need human love and fellowship, and a heavenly Father's care; and narrow enough to shut out all envy, pride, and hate. Make its threshold smooth enough to be no stumbling block to children, nor to straying feet, but rugged enough to turn back the tempter's power: make it a gateway to thine eternal kingdom.

Bishop Thomas Ken (1637–1711)

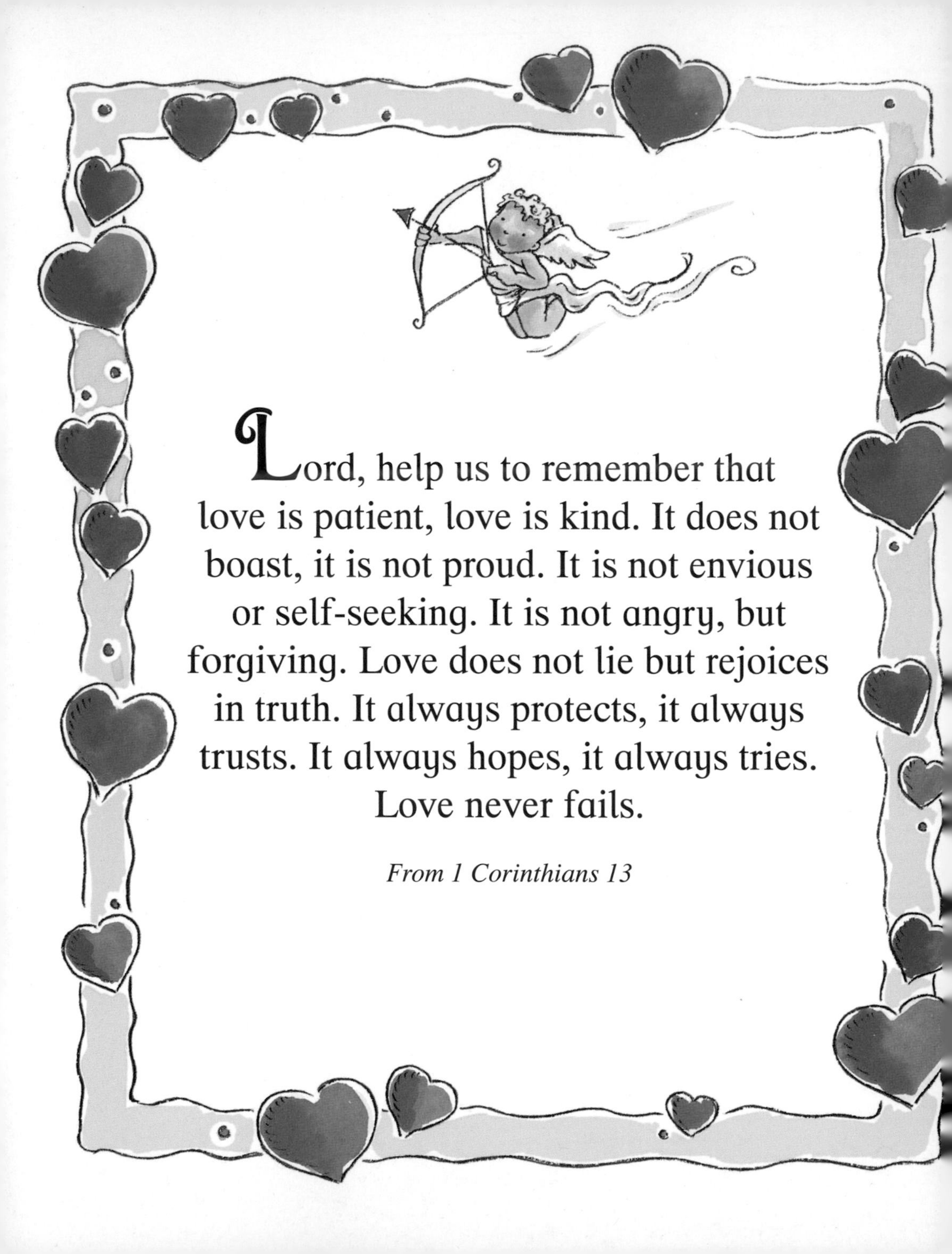

Lord, help us to remember that love is patient, love is kind. It does not boast, it is not proud. It is not envious or self-seeking. It is not angry, but forgiving. Love does not lie but rejoices in truth. It always protects, it always trusts. It always hopes, it always tries. Love never fails.

From 1 Corinthians 13

God bless you,
God bless me,
And keep us safe
As safe can be.

Dear Lord Jesus, when you came into the world you had no home. Mary and Joseph had to travel to a strange town and lay you in a manger in a stable. Please help all the people who are homeless today or who have to travel far from their homes. Help us think about how we, who have homes, can help them and remember them.

Thank you for visits
And all kinds of treats.
Thank you for walking
Down different streets.
Thank you for good times
Wherever we roam.
But most of all, God,
Thank you for home.

Jesus bless our home today,
Be known in all we do and say.
When there's trouble, be our guide,
Bless everyone who steps inside.

Jesus said, "Let the little children come to me, for the kingdom of God belongs to such as these."

Matthew 19:14; Mark 10:14; Luke 18:16

Dear Lord, I love my little bed
Where I can lay my tired head.
It's great to have a place to be
Where there is only you and me.

God bless this mess,
But make me strong
To put things back
Where they belong!

God bless Mom and Dad
For all the good times we have had;
For vacations, birthdays, holiday fun;
For games and races that I won!

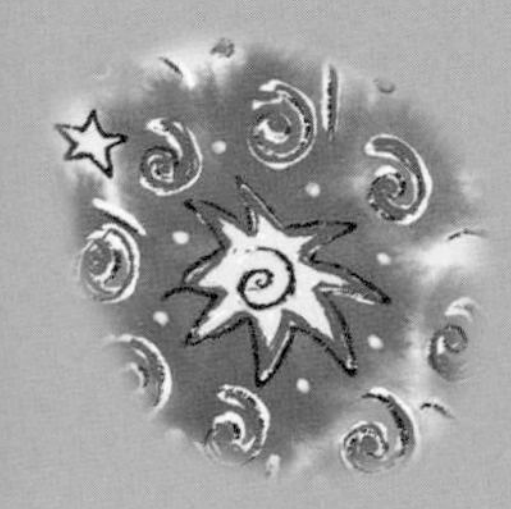

For afternoons spent in the park;
For watching fireworks after dark;
For all the stories they have read
At night, when I go up to bed.

Keep them safe, oh Lord, I pray,
So I can love them every day.

God bless all those that I love.
God bless all those that love me.
God bless all those that love those that I love,
And all those that love those that love me.

From an old New England sampler

My mom does so many special things,
There's no end to the joy she brings.
She buys my clothes, cooks food I like,
She comforts me when I fall off my bike.
I love her more than I can say
And try to show her every day!

When we go out my dad says,
"Son, don't run,

Look around you, listen hard,
Walk, don't talk."

We see everything all around us
From trees to bees.

Thank you, God, for my dad.
Tell him I love him.

Dear Father, when we've had a bad day and all said things we didn't mean, help us not to let the sun go down before we've made things right again. Help me take the first step and say, "I'm sorry."

Dear God, I love to help my dad in the garden. There's a lot to be done, and it's hard work, but I don't mind at all because we're doing it together, which makes it fun.

Hush my dear, lie still and slumber
Holy angels guard thy bed,
Heavenly blessings without number
Gently falling on thy head.

Dr. Isaac Watts (1674–1748)

We've got a new baby. It's part of our family now. When it holds my hand, and when it smiles at me, I like it very much.

We've got a new baby.
It's hungry all the time.
When it makes a smell and cries
and cries, I don't like it at all.

Thank you for our new baby. On bad days and good; it's part of our family now, and I love it.

Dear God, first there was only me and my mom and dad, but now I've got a baby brother. He gets lots of attention and he cries a lot. Sometimes I feel a bit left out, and then I wish he hadn't come along. But he giggles when I play with him, so I think he's going to turn out OK.

Dear God, I do love my brother but I don't always like him. Sometimes we fight and do mean things to each other. Help me remember that, even when I don't like him, I still love him.

Dear God,
You won't be pleased
With what I did today.
My sister tried to kiss me
But I turned my face away.
Please tell her that I love her
And I'm really going to try
To be a lot more loving,
But it's hard because I'm shy.

Dear God, help me love the people in my family even when I don't like them.

Thank you God for all the different
People you created
And thank you, most of all, for those
To whom I am related.

I live for those who love me,
Whose hearts are kind and true;
For the heaven that smiles above me,
And awaits my spirit too;
For all human ties that bind me,
For the task my God assigned me,
For the bright hopes left behind me,
And the good that I can do.

George Linnaeus Banks (1821–1881)

Thank you for Gran,
Who does what she can
When we go to her place.
Thank you for Grandpa,
Who knows where the treats are
And always says grace.

Grandpa's got a crazy cat
That jumps up on the chairs,
And mom says he looks untidy
In the battered hat he wears.

But Grandpa's really funny;
He takes me out for walks,
He tells fantastic stories
And we have important talks.

So thank you God for Grandpa
With his funny battered hat.
Please tell him that I love him,
And I even love his cat!

Thank you Lord for grandmas and grandpas. Thank you for the stories they tell us and the things they help us make. Thank you that they have time to tie our shoelaces and take us for walks. Please bless them all.

Grandma sits me on her knee,
Strokes my hair and sings to me.
Grandpa jokes and likes to play ball,
And picks me up when I fall.

At dinner Grandpa likes to cook
While Grandma sits and reads a book.
I love them, Lord, and pray that they
Will be there for me every day.

My mom's mom is called my grandma. My mom's mom's mom is my great grandma. Even though she's very old, she talks to me and remembers my name. She IS great!

Please God, bless my really great grandma.

Dear God, bless all the children who have no family. Please look after them and send them someone who will care for them so that they will not be alone.

God bless all the aunts
Who are kind to girls and boys;
God bless all the uncles
Who remember birthday toys.

My aunt and uncle live very far away. I never see them, but they write me letters and send a card for my birthday. Thank you that they think of me and that they send their love right around the world.

I'm glad I've got an aunt,
She really is a winner.
She takes me out to feed the ducks,
And then she makes me dinner.

She shows me all the photographs
Of when she and Mom were young.
I thank you, God, that Aunt and me
Have loads and loads of fun.

Dear God, we like our cousins.
When they come to stay,
We talk and laugh and run and jump
And play.

Then we have an argument,
We shout and yell and fight.
We want them to go home again
That night.

But when they've gone we're sorry,
Although they are a pain,
We miss them and we cannot wait till they come
Back again!

Dear God, sometimes we have family arguments. When we do, help us remember that we love each other really. Help us be quick to make up.

Dear Father God, my mom and dad have split up, and now I have two families. It's sometimes hard because I try to keep everyone happy. Please be with us all as we try to work it out.

Dear God, thank you for my family and the things we do together. Thank you for the meals we eat, for the jokes we share, for the TV we watch, for the place where we live. Help us remember that we are part of your family.

Look after my family when we have to be apart. Thank you for the thoughts we share, the phone calls we make, the messages we send, the memories we keep, the prayers we pray. Help us remember that you are with us all.

Dear Father, I pray today for
all of my friends.

Here are their names:

....

....

....

Dear Father, thank you for my friends.
Help me be a good friend to them.
Bless them and keep them safe,
today and always.

Lord behold our family here assembled.
We thank thee for this place in which we dwell; for the love that unites us; for the peace accorded us this day; for the hope with which we expect the morrow; for the health, the work, the food, and the bright skies that make our life delightful; for our friends in all parts of the earth.
Let peace abound in our small community.
Give us courage, gaiety, and the quiet mind.

Robert Louis Stevenson (1850–1894)

Dear God, I kept a caterpillar
in a jar and it went into a little
black cocoon. I thought it
was dead. But later, out of
the cocoon came a beautiful
butterfly. Help me remember
that people who die are a bit
like my caterpillar. In your
home in heaven, they will
be happy again like
beautiful butterflies.

Dear God,
If you are listening,
My grandma died last night.
Mom says she's gone to heaven,
And dad said, "Yes, that's right."
So God, if you should see her
In heaven up on high,
Please tell her that I'll miss her
And I'm trying not to cry.

Thank you,
God, that everyone belongs
to your family; you are our
Father, we are your children.
Thank you, God, for the
worldwide family of your people.
Thank you for our brothers
and sisters the whole
world over.

Neighbors, everybody needs good neighbors.
Please God bless mine, and help me be a
good neighbor, too.

We commend unto you, Oh Lord,
our souls and our bodies, our minds and our
thoughts, our prayers and our hopes, our health
and our work, our life and our death, our parents
and brothers and sisters, our benefactors and
friends, our neighbors, our countrymen, and
all Christian folk, this day and always.

Lancelot Andrews (1555–1626)

Father God, bless me and my family.
Dear Jesus, keep my family and me.
Holy Spirit, guard us all.
Great God, keep us in the circle
of your love.

Jesus, friend of little children,
Be a friend to me;
Take my hand, and ever keep me
Close to thee.

Never leave me, nor forsake me;
Ever be my friend;
For I need thee, from life's dawning
To its end.

Walter J. Mathams (1851–1931)

You made the people that I meet,
The many people, great and small,
In home and school and down the street,
And you made me to love them all.

J. M. C. Crum (adapted)

Josie is my best friend;
She's never rude or cruel.
Jimmy is the tallest,
And he thinks he's really cool.
Jason wears a white shirt,
And gets his math all right.
Alice is the sweetest,
Her curls are small and tight.
All my friends are special,
They mean a lot to me.
And Jesus is my friend as well
Because he cares for me.

Sometimes I'm up, sometimes down,
My thoughts are like a seesaw.
But I thank God you're always there—
That's what friends are for.

The Bible says, don't let the sun go down on your anger. Dear Lord, when I have a fight with my friend, help us make up before we leave each other, because it will be much harder to say sorry the next day.

Oh God,
I feel so bad,
I said some things
I shouldn't have.
I want to start
Again and say
With all my heart
I'm sorry.

Love is giving, not taking,
Mending, not breaking,
Trusting, believing,
Never deceiving,
Patiently bearing
And faithfully sharing
Each joy, every sorrow,
Today and tomorrow.

Anonymous

Love is giving your last treat to a friend.
Dear God, help me love like that.

Two of us sharing,
Two of us caring.
Nothing is better,
In all kinds of weather.

Dear God, thank you for giving me friends of all different shapes and sizes. We come from different homes, and speak different languages. But when we share our thoughts and hopes and fears we find we're really not that different after all.

Dear God, I don't like changes! My friend is going away. I'm so sad; I don't know what I'll do without her. I know she is feeling sad, too. As we remember the good times we've had together, help us let each other go. We'll always remember each other and keep in touch, but we also have to make new friends.

May our friendship last
though we are apart.
May our friendship last
when we are busy.
May our friendship last
even when we make new ones.
May our friendship last
as long as we live.

Anonymous

Thank you, God, for my friends at church. We are all different ages and shapes and sizes, but we are all part of your family.

Dear God, thank you for our neighbors, who come from so many different places to live near us. Help us make them our friends, too.

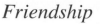

May the road rise to meet you.
May the wind be always at your back.
May the sun shine warm upon your face,
the rains fall soft upon your fields,
and, until we meet again, may God
hold you in the palm of his hand.

Irish blessing

All people that on earth do dwell,
Sing to the Lord with cheerful voice;
Him serve with mirth, his praise forth tell;
Come ye before him and rejoice.

Scottish Psalter (1650)

Father God, who gave me life,
help me live for you.

Teach me, my God and king,
In all things thee to see,
That what I do in anything
To do it as for thee.

George Herbert (1593–1632)

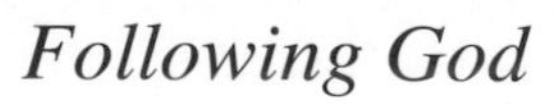

What can I give him,
Poor as I am?
If I were a shepherd,
I would bring him a lamb.

If I were a wise man,
I would do my part—
Yet what I can I give him:
Give him my heart.

Christina Rossetti (1830–1894)

Teach us, Lord, to serve you as you deserve, to give and not to count the cost, to fight and not to heed the wounds, to toil and not to seek for rest, to labor and not to ask for any reward save that of knowing that we do your will.

St. Ignatius Loyola (1491–1556)

Guide us, teach us, and strengthen us, oh Lord, we beseech thee, until we become such as thou would'st have us be: pure, gentle, truthful, high-minded, courteous, generous, able, dutiful, and useful; for thy honor and glory.

Charles Kingsley (1819–1875)

Lord, teach me all that I should know;
In grace and wisdom I may grow;
The more I learn to do thy will,
The better may I love thee still.

Isaac Watts (1674–1748)

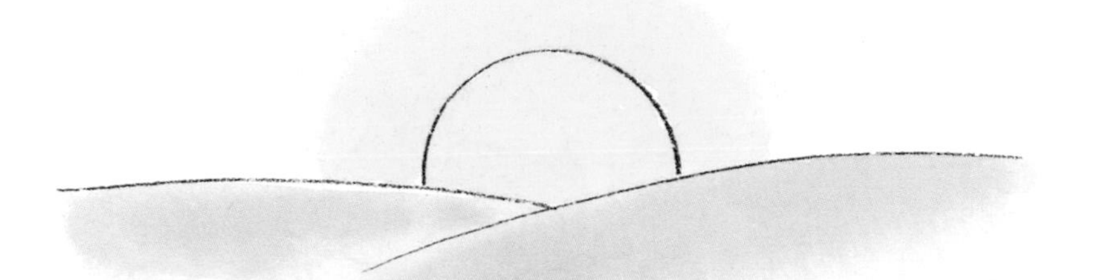

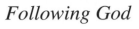

Day by day, dear Lord, of thee
Three things I pray:
To see thee more clearly,
To love thee more dearly,
To follow thee more nearly,
Day by day.

St. Richard of Chichester (1197–1253)

Every day with Jesus
Is a special day.
Jesus, help me always
To walk your way.

Every day I thank you Lord,
I'm very glad I live,
Help me to pass on the joy
That knowing you can give.

Father, help me see the world as you see it,
help me live in the world as you would live,
help me care about the world in all its troubles,
help me play my part in making it better.

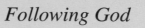

Oh God, make us children of quietness and heirs of peace.

St. Clement

Make me pure, Lord: thou art holy;
Make me meek, Lord: thou wert lowly.

Gerard Manley Hopkins (1844–1889)

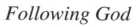

God our Father, creator of the world,
please help us love one another.
Make nations friendly with other nations;
make all of us love one another like brothers
and sisters. Help us do our part to bring peace
in the world and happiness to all people.

Prayer from Japan

Last night, when I went to sleep,
I prayed that you would help me keep
A promise that I made to Mom
Not to be so quarrelsome.

I've really tried so hard today
To keep the promise, come what may.
And, Jesus, you will never guess
I think I've done it, more or less!

Dear God,
I think I'll help more
And give my mom some pleasure.
I'll straighten up my bedroom
And be her "little treasure."

I offer thee
Every flower that ever grew,
Every bird that ever flew,
Every wind that ever blew,
Good God.

I offer thee
Every flake of virgin snow,
Every spring of earth below,
Every human joy and woe,
My Love!

Irish prayer

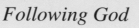

Dear God,
when I feel like a nobody,
help me remember that
I am somebody to you.

Do other children help much?
Please tell me if they do,
And I'll make a special effort
For Mom and Dad and you.

Lord, make my heart a place
where angels sing!

John Keble (1792–1866)

Oh make my heart so still, so still,
When I am deep in prayer,
That I might hear the white mist-wreaths
Losing themselves in air!

Utsonomya San, Japan

Dear God,
I'm going to really try
To be good as gold all day,
And nice to all my special friends
When I go out to play.
If they say nasty things to me
I mustn't do the same.
I don't want Mom to get annoyed,
Or worse—give me the blame!
But, God, it isn't easy
To be as nice as pie,
So I know that you will help me
To really, really try!

Dear God, I love secrets.
Help me know when I should keep a secret and when I should tell a secret.
And help me understand the difference between the two.

Move our hearts with the calm, smooth flow of your grace. Let the river of your love run through our souls. May my soul be carried by the current of your love, toward the wide, infinite ocean of heaven.

Gilbert of Hoyland (12th century)

This is me
looking up at you.
Help me always be
close to you.

Jesus, may I
Walk your way
(point to feet)

In all I do
(hold out hands)

And all I say.
(touch finger to lips)

Oh gracious and holy Father,
give us wisdom to perceive thee, intelligence
to understand thee, diligence to seek thee,
patience to wait for thee, eyes to behold
thee, a heart to meditate upon thee, and a
life to proclaim thee; through the power
of the Spirit of Jesus Christ our Lord.

St. Benedict (480–543)

Teach me to do the thing that's right,
And when I sin, forgive,
And make it still my chief delight
To serve thee while I live.

Jane Taylor (1783–1824)

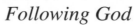

Help me notice when people need a hand. Help me see when they are sad and need a friend.

Dear God, today started badly and got worse, like a drawing that went wrong. Help me bring the drawing to you so that you can rub it out and give me a clean sheet of paper for tomorrow.

Sometimes I'm good,
But I can be bad.
Sometimes I'm happy,
Sometimes I'm sad.

I can be helpful,
I can be mean.
Sometimes I'm somewhere
In between.
Help me do what I know I should do.
Help me choose to be good like you.

Gentle Jesus, hear me,
Will you please be near me,
I don't want to be alone,
Feeling sad all on my own.
Tomorrow will be different
At the start of a new day,
But until the morning comes,
Stay close to me, I pray.

Oh God, as truly as you are
our father, so just as truly you are
our mother. We thank you, God our
father, for your strength and goodness.
We thank you, God our mother,
for the closeness of your caring.
Oh God, we thank you for the great
love you have for each one of us.

Julian of Norwich (1343–1413)

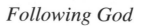

Oh God, help us not to despise or oppose what we do not understand.

William Penn (1644–1718)

Help me to know
What's wrong and what's right;
Help me to do good
With all my might.

Dear God,
Help me to be good
When I have to share my toys.
Help me to be good
When I'm making too much noise.
Help me to be good
And eat up all my greens.
Help me to be good
When I'm tempted to be mean.
Help me to be good
Each and every day.
Help me to be good
In every single way.

When I feel blue,
Give me something to do
For somebody else
Who is feeling sad, too.

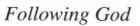

When I feel small and quite alone,
I know I'm not.
Because, dear God, I know you're there—
It helps a lot!

Now thank we all our God
With hearts and hands and voices
Who wondrous things hath done,
In whom this world rejoices;
Who from our mother's arms
Hath blessed us on our way
With countless gifts of love,
And still is ours today.

Martin Rinkart (1586–1649)

Good Morning

Our Father in heaven,
Hallowed be your name.
Your kingdom come,
Your will be done,
On earth as it is in heaven.
Give us today our daily bread,
And forgive us our sins,
As we forgive those who sin against us.
Lead us away from temptation
And deliver us from evil,
For yours is the kingdom,
And the power, and the glory,
Forever and ever.
Amen

The prayer that Jesus taught his friends

My Father, for another night
Of quiet sleep and rest,
For all the joy of morning light,
Your holy name be blest.

Henry William Baker (1821–1877)

In the quiet of the morning,
be still and know that God is near.

Adapted from Psalm 46

Something's gone wrong with this morning,
My pillow seems stuck to my head!
I'm in a bad mood,
I've gone right off my food,
And I don't want to get out of bed.

Dear God, can you help with this morning?
I really don't want to be sad.
Though the morning is gray,
This is a new day,
So perhaps things aren't really so bad!

Whatever I do and wherever I go, be with me, Lord, this day.

Lord, be with us this day.
Within us to purify us;
above us to draw us up;
beneath us to sustain us;
before us to lead us;
behind us to restrain us;
around us to protect us.

St. Patrick (389–461)

Good morning, good morning,
Praise to you each morning,
Good morning, good morning to you!

All that we see rejoices in the sunshine,
All that we hear makes merry in the spring:
God grant us such a mind
To be glad after our kind,
And to sing his praises evermore for everything.

Christina Rossetti (1830–1894)

I go forth today
in the might of heaven,
in the brightness of the sun,
in the whiteness of snow,
in the splendor of fire,
in the speed of lightning,
in the swiftness of wind,
in the firmness of rock.
I go forth today
in the hand of God.

Irish prayer (8th century)

Christ be with me and within me;
Christ behind me;
Christ to win me;
Christ to comfort and restore me;
Christ beneath me;
Christ above me;
Christ in quiet and in danger;
Christ in hearts of all that love me;
Christ in mouth of friend and stranger.

St. Patrick (389–461)

This is the day that the Lord has made,
I will rejoice and be glad in it.

From Psalm 118:24

The rooster crows at break of day,
"What a wonderful world!" he seems to say.
When I awake, although I'm yawning,
I thank the Lord for a brand new morning.

God be in my head, and in my understanding; God be in my eyes, and in my looking; God be in my mouth, and in my speaking; God be in my heart, and in my thinking; God be at my end, and at my departing.

The Sarum Primer

Oh great Chief, light a candle within my heart that I may see what is therein and sweep the rubbish from your dwelling place.

Prayer from Africa

Can I see another's woe,
And not be in sorrow, too?
Can I see another's grief,
And not seek for kind relief?

William Blake (1757–1827)

Let the words of my mouth,
and the meditation of my heart,
be acceptable in thy sight, Oh Lord,
my strength, and my redeemer.

From Psalm 19

Come into my soul, Lord,
as the dawn breaks into the sky;
let your sun rise in my heart
at the coming of the day.

Traditional

This is the morning, clear and bright,
This is the break of day.
This is the last gray strands of night,
This is the time to pray.

Holy, holy, holy, Lord God almighty!
Early in the morning our song shall rise to thee.

Bishop Herbert (1782–1826)

God, who has folded back the mantle of the night to clothe us in the golden glory of the day, chase from our hearts all gloomy thoughts and make us glad with the brightness of hope.

Book of Common Prayer

Dear God, this is a new day.
Help me learn from yesterday's
mistakes and do better today.

I've washed my face
And brushed my teeth
And combed my hair right through,
And so dear Lord
I'm ready now
To face this day with you.

I bind unto myself today
The power of God to hold and lead,
His eye to watch, his might to stay,
His ear to hearken to my need;
The wisdom of my God to teach,
His hand to guide, his shield to ward;
The word of God to give me speech,
His heavenly host to be my guard.

St. Patrick (389–461)

Dear God, please bless
In park or street
The people I see.
Dear God, this day
Bless me to them
And them to me.

Traditional

Dear God, this is Monday.
Help me start a good week.

Dear God, it's Tuesday.
It's still early in the week.
Be with me as I try to make it
a good one.

Dear God, it's Friday.
Nearly the weekend! Time to look back on my week. Thank you for being with me.

Dear God, it's Saturday—yippeee!
So much to do, so little time.
Please bless all my friends today.

Dear God, it's Sunday, your day. Happy day. Holy day. Thank you for the past week. Please help me enjoy next week with you.

Sunday should be a fun day,
Not a glum day.
Sunday should be a rest day,
Not a work day.

When God finished making the world,
he had a rest, put up his feet,
and said, “That’s good!”
Dear God, thank you for this Sunday.
Help us rest and play, celebrate
and say, “That’s good!”

Here is the church, *(link hands)*

Here is the steeple, *(put index fingers together)*

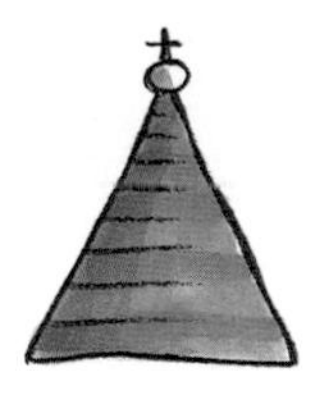

Look inside, *(keeping your hands linked, turn them upside down)*

Here are the people! *(wiggle your fingers)*

Traditional

Bless the bride and bless the groom
In every kind of weather.
Bless their love and bless their home
And all their life together.

Special baby, we gather around
to welcome you into God's family,
the church.

We will always be here for you
as brothers and sisters and
children of God.

Lord Jesus, thank you for making me.
Thank you for loving me, thank you for
calling me to follow you.
In this confirmation service, I give
myself back to you in love and joy.
Help me to live for you and for others
with the help of your Holy Spirit,
today and every day.

Lord, you know that we are sad today because someone we loved very much has died. Today is a day to say goodbye and to hand them into your care. Help us to know that they are at peace with you, and that one day we will see them again in heaven.

These candles on my cake,
I blow them out,
A wish I make.
To this wish
I add a prayer:
Please God, be with me
Everywhere.

We're off on vacation. Oh what fun!
There may be rain or there may be sun.
But we'll all have a lovely time together,
And thank you, God, whatever the weather!

Today is a day to remember—
I finally pulled out my loose tooth!
I feel more grown-up already.
Thank you, God, for special
days to remember.

We've been packing our stuff,
We've been counting the days,
We've been saying goodbye
In a whole lot of ways.
It's a very special day—we're moving!

Please travel with us
As we leave our old home,
Please help us to know
That we're never alone.
It's a very special day—WE'RE MOVING!

Come, thou long-expected Jesus,
Born to set thy people free,
From our fears and sins release us,
Let us find our rest in thee.

Charles Wesley (1707–1788)

Away in a manger, no crib for a bed,
The little Lord Jesus laid down his sweet head.
The stars in the bright sky looked down where he lay,
The little Lord Jesus asleep on the hay.

Be near me, Lord Jesus; I ask thee to stay
Close by me forever, and love me, I pray.
Bless all the dear children in thy tender care,
And fit us for heaven, to live with thee there.

Traditional

Happy Birthday, Jesus!
Thank you for sharing your special day
with us. The kings brought you gifts,
so we give presents. Your family was happy,
so we have parties and food.
Thank you for giving us Christmas.
Happy Birthday, Jesus!

Love came down at Christmas,
Love all lovely, love divine;
Love was born at Christmas,
Star and angels gave the sign.

Christina Rossetti (1830–1894)

Lord Jesus, wise men brought
you gifts when you were born:
gold, frankincense, and myrrh.
They were a sign that you would
be a king, a prophet, and a savior.
Thank you for the presents
we give each other at Christmas.
May they always be a sign of love.

Dear God, as I stand at the door
Of this new year with you,
Help me to take your hand
And to walk through,
Trusting that you
Will be with me always
In everything I think
And do and say.

This is a time for giving things up,
so we remember how many good
things we have.

This is a time for taking things up,
so we remember to give good things
to others.

Pancakes are yummy, but after today
We won't eat pancakes for many a day.
We're taking some time out
To think about things,
And we're waiting for Easter
When everyone sings.
Hallelujah!

Ash gray,
Sad day,
Time to make amends
For all the things
We've failed to do
For family and friends.

Ash gray,
Hopeful day,
Thank you, God, that you
Forgive our sins
And give us time
To go and live for you.

Dear Lord Jesus, thank you for the special meal that you shared with your friends before you died on the cross. You took bread and said it was like your own body. You took wine, like your own blood, and invited them to share it with you. Thank you that we can share the same meal so many years later, and become your friends as well.

Dear Jesus, everyone thought you were dead. They took you down from the cross, with tears in their eyes, and buried you in a cave with a big stone outside. Then they went home—the saddest people on earth.

Later, they went back to take flowers, but they got such a shock. The stone was rolled away, the cave was empty, and you were walking in the garden. Then they were the happiest people on earth. No wonder we are happy at Easter. We know that you're alive and always will be.

Jesus, who died for me,
Help me to live for thee.

Holy Spirit, hear me,
Friend from heaven above,
You are ever near me,
Fill my heart with love.

God the Father, bless us;
God the Son, defend us;
God the Spirit, keep us now
and evermore.

A Celtic blessing

God bless my dad,
So strong and tall:
The bestest daddy
Of them all.

This is the thing
I want to say,
I love him loads
On Father's Day.

All the children of the world are friends,
so let us be friendly together, learn the
will of God, and do our best this day.
All the children of the world are friends.
Let us sing together joyously; let us praise
God loudly all this day.

Japanese prayer

Each day is new-baked, like a loaf of bread.
May we take it, smell it, taste and enjoy it,
and give thanks to the one who made it for us.

Start each day with a fresh beginning;
as if this whole world was made anew.

From an Amish school

Now the light has gone away,
Savior, listen while I pray,
Asking thee to watch and keep,
And to send me quiet sleep.

Frances Ridley Havergal (1836–1879)

Sleep, my child, and peace attend thee,
All through the night;
Guardian angels God will send thee,
All through the night.
Soft the drowsy hours are creeping,
Hill and vale in slumber sleeping,
I my loving vigil keeping,
All through the night.

Traditional Welsh prayer

Lord, when we have not any light,
And mothers are asleep,
Then through the stillness of the night
Thy little children keep.

When shadows haunt the quiet room,
Help us to understand
That thou art with us through the gloom,
To hold us by the hand.

Anne Matheson (1853–1924)

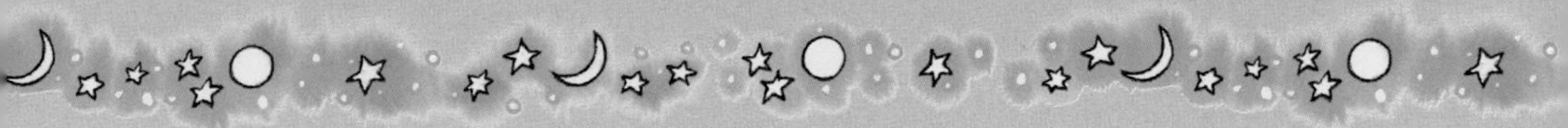

When in the night I sleepless lie,
My soul with heavenly thoughts supply;
Let no ill dreams disturb my rest,
No powers of darkness me molest.

Bishop Thomas Ken (1637–1711)

Jesus, savior, wash away
All that has been wrong today:
Help me every day to be
Good and gentle, more like thee.

Frances Ridley Havergal (1836–1879)

Jesus tender shepherd, hear me,
Bless your little lamb tonight;
Through the darkness please be near me;
Keep me safe till morning light.

Mary Lundie Duncan (1814–1840)

Now I lay me down to sleep,
I pray the Lord my soul to keep.
If I should die before I wake,
I pray the Lord my soul to take.

Traditional

Lord, keep us safe this night,
Secure from all our fears;
May angels guard us while we sleep,
Till morning light appears.

John Leland (1754–1841)

God bless this house
From roof to floor,
The twelve apostles guard the door;
Four angels to my bed;
Gabriel stands at the head,
John and Peter at the feet,
All to watch me while I sleep.

Traditional

Father God, as the sun goes down and I get ready for bed, other children around the world are just waking up. As you are with me through this night, please be with them in their day.

Around our pillows golden ladders rise,
And up and down the skies,
With winged sandals shod,
The angels come and go;
The messengers of God!

Richard Henry Stoddard (1825–1903)

Matthew, Mark, Luke, and John,
Bless the bed that I lie on.
Four corners to my bed,
Four angels round my head,
One to watch and one to pray
And two to bear my soul away.

Traditional

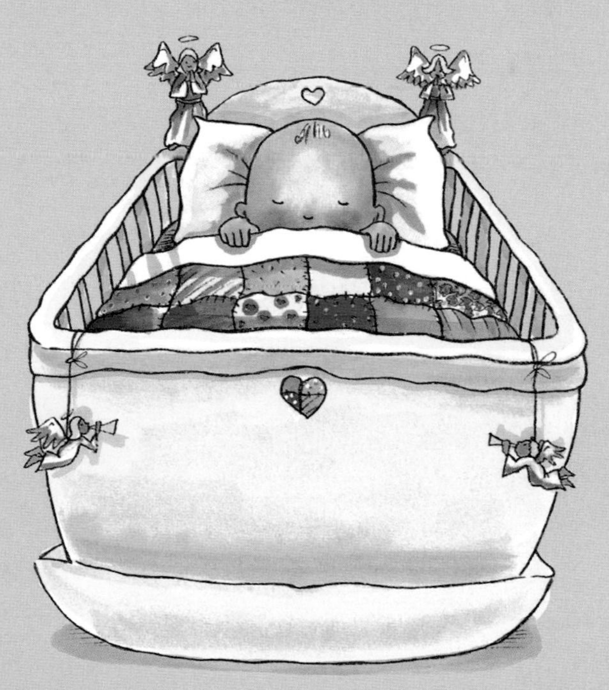

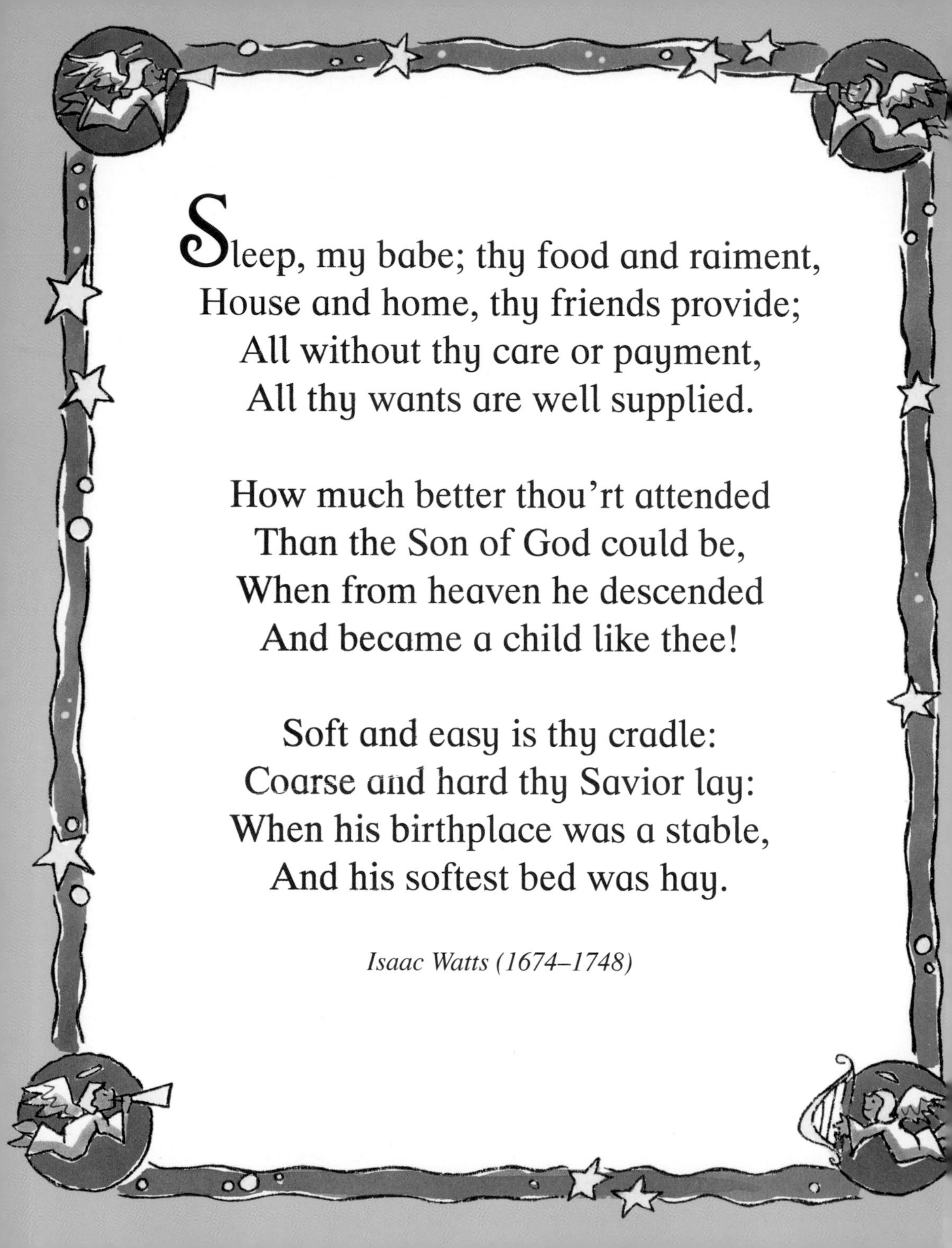

Sleep, my babe; thy food and raiment,
House and home, thy friends provide;
All without thy care or payment,
All thy wants are well supplied.

How much better thou'rt attended
Than the Son of God could be,
When from heaven he descended
And became a child like thee!

Soft and easy is thy cradle:
Coarse and hard thy Savior lay:
When his birthplace was a stable,
And his softest bed was hay.

Isaac Watts (1674–1748)

Keep watch, dear Lord, with those who work, or watch, or weep this night, and give your angels charge over those who sleep.

St. Augustine (354–430)

When I lie down, I go to sleep in peace; you alone, oh Lord, keep me perfectly safe.

From Psalm 4

Thank you God for a lovely day,
For sun and rain,
For work and play,
For all my family
And friends,
And for your love,
Which never ends.

Good night! Good night!
Far flies the light;
But still God's love
Shall flame above,
Making all bright.
Good night! Good night!

Victor Hugo (1802–1885)

Ah, dearest Jesus, holy child,
Make thee a bed, soft, undefiled
Within my heart, that it may be
A quiet chamber kept for thee.

Martin Luther (1483–1546)

I see the moon,
And the moon sees me;
God bless the moon
And God bless me.
Anonymous

The moon shines bright,
The stars give light
Before the break of day;
God bless you all,
Both great and small,
And send a joyful day.

Traditional

Dear God,
I'm staying over with my friend tonight,
We'll have a terrific time and not fight.
We'll eat too much, we'll jump on beds and have a lark
So when you come to look for me and it's dark,
I won't be in my bed,
I'll be with my friend instead.

I'm sleeping at my grandma's
And I miss my mom and dad.
But Grandma cooked my favorite dinner
And now I'm not so sad!

I like to sleep at Grandma's;
She says it makes her glad.
Please, God, bless my grandma
And bless my mom and dad.

God bless Dad,
God bless Mom,
God bless me
and everyone.

Dear Father, thank you for today. There were good parts I'd like to remember and bad parts I'd rather forget. Forgive me for the things I did wrong and help me to be better tomorrow. Thank you for all the good things and thank you for being with me in it all.

God bless everyone in
the whole wide world tonight.
Guard us and guide us and help
us love one another, so that your
world can be a happy and peaceful
place for all people.

Day is done,
Gone the sun
From the lake,
From the hills,
From the sky.
Safely rest,
All is well!
God is nigh.

Traditional

Sleep little baby,
Soundly sleep,
Safe in my arms
My watch I'll keep,

And wing my prayer
To God above,
Who watches over us
With love.

Tend your sick ones, oh Lord Jesus Christ; rest your weary ones; bless your dying ones; soothe your suffering ones; pity your afflicted ones; shield your joyous ones; and all for your love's sake.

St. Augustine (354–430)

When I put my hands together,
When I say a prayer,
When I stop and say your name
You are there.

When I'm frightened of the dark,
When I've had a scare,
When I think I'm all alone
You are there.

Jesus, please be near me
As I lie in bed tonight,
There's a dark place in the corner
And it's giving me a fright!
Mom says it's just a shadow,
And shadows are thin air,
But I can see it grinning,
And it's sitting in my chair!
Please shine your light, dear Jesus,
So that I can see
The shadow's really nothing
Now that you are close to me.

Alone with none but thee, my God,
I journey on my way.
What need I fear, when thou art near
Oh king of night and day?
More safe am I within thy hand
Than if a host did round me stand.

St. Columba (521–597)

Send peace into my heart, oh Lord,
that I may be contented with your mercies
of this day and confident of your protection for
this night; and having forgiven others, even as
you forgive me, may I go to my rest in peaceful
trust through Jesus Christ our Lord.

St. Francis of Assisi (1181–1226)

Peace of the running waves to you,
Deep peace of the flowing air to you,
Deep peace of the quiet earth to you,
Deep peace of the shining stars to you,
Deep peace of the shades of night to you,
Moon and stars always giving light to you.
Deep peace of Christ, the Son of Peace, to you.

Traditional Gaelic blessing

Glory be to thee, my God, this night,
For all the blessings of the light;
Keep me, oh keep me, king of kings,
Beneath thine own almighty wings.

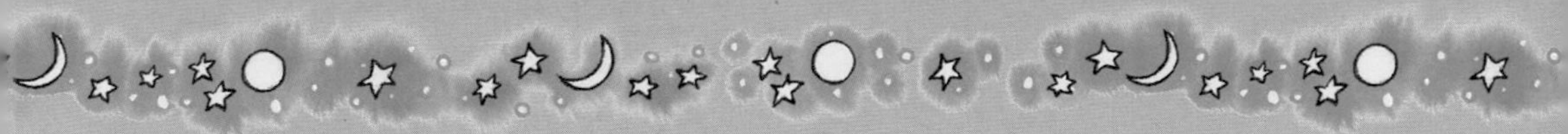

In peace I will both lie down and sleep, for you alone, oh Lord, make me to dwell in safety.

From Psalm 4

Give me peace in my heart, keep me praying,
Give me peace in my heart, I pray,
Give me peace in my heart, keep me praying,
Keep me praying till the end of day.

Traditional

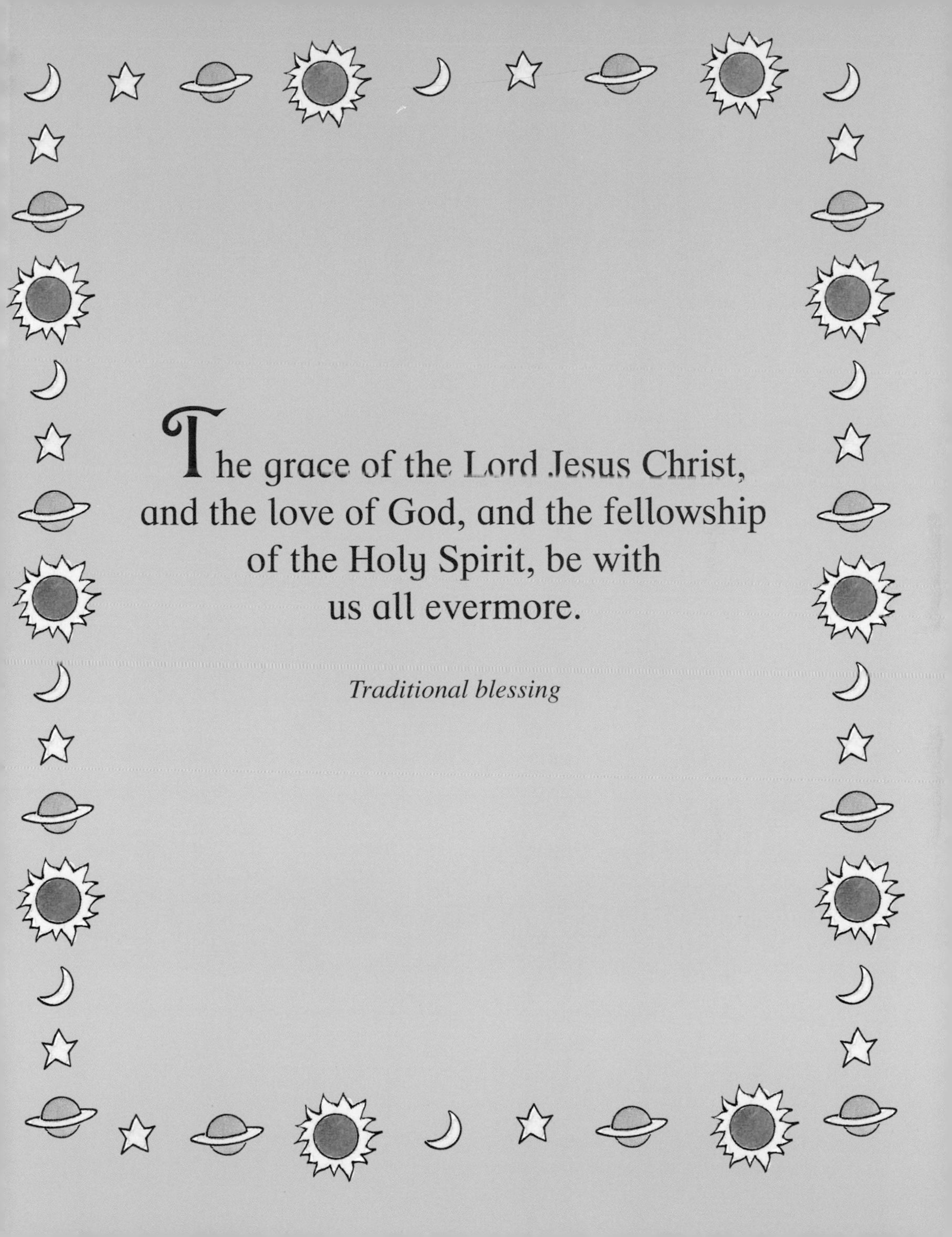

The grace of the Lord Jesus Christ, and the love of God, and the fellowship of the Holy Spirit, be with us all evermore.

Traditional blessing

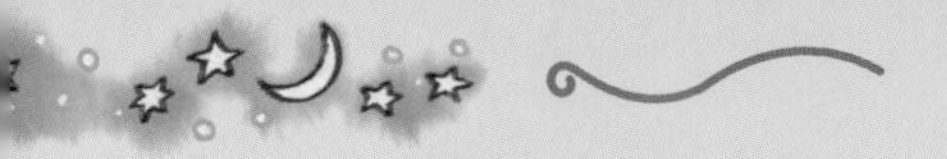

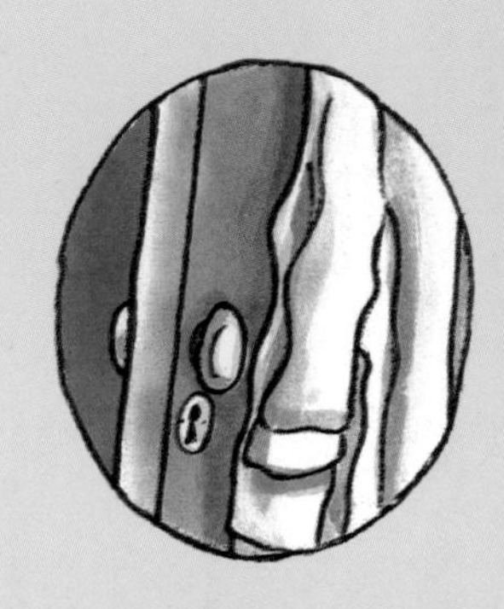

It's time to sleep.
I've brushed my teeth
And read my book,
I've put my bathrobe
On the hook,
And ...

I just can't sleep.
The bed's too hot,
The light's too bright,
There are far too many
Sounds tonight,
But ...

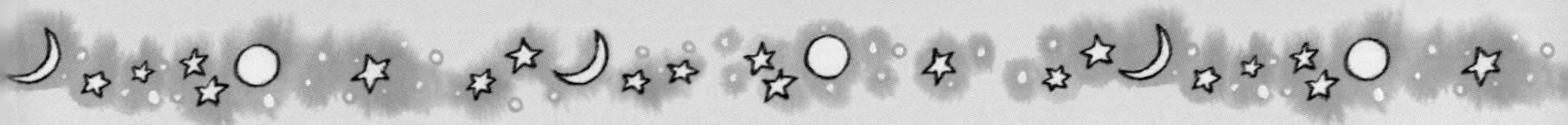

I still can't sleep.
I've shut my eyes,
I've said a prayer,
"God bless children
Everywhere,"
Then ...

Maybe I'll sleep.
I think I might,
I think I'll—yawn—
turn out the light.
Good night.
Zzzzz ...

Index of First Lines